Joke & Riddle GOLD MINE

MICHAEL J. PELLOWSKI

STERLING CHILDREN'S BOOKS
New York

To Heidi Goldberg and Lauren Altman
Always Remembered

STERLING CHILDREN'S BOOKS
New York

An Imprint of Sterling Publishing Co., Inc.
1166 Avenue of the Americas
New York, NY 10036

ISBN 978-1-4549-2228-5

Distributed in Canada by Sterling Publishing Co., Inc.
c/o Canadian Manda Group, 664 Annette Street
Toronto, Ontario, Canada M6S 2C8
Distributed in the United Kingdom by GMC Distribution Services
Castle Place, 166 High Street, Lewes, East Sussex, England BN7 1XU
Distributed in Australia by NewSouth Books
45 Beach Street, Coogee, NSW 2034, Australia

For information about custom editions, special sales, and premium and corporate
purchases, please contact Sterling Special Sales at 800-805-5489
or specialsales@sterlingpublishing.com.

Manufactured in Canada
Lot #:
2 4 6 8 10 9 7 5 3 1
01/17

www.sterlingpublishing.com

Design by Ryan Thomann

Contents

HA HA HA HA

1

Which fish won first place on a TV reality show?

The sole survivor.

Knock-knock!

Who's there?

I, Nemo.

I, Nemo who?

I Nemo money, so lend me some.

What did Mr. Sea Sponge say to the big bully?

"Leave me alone, or I'll wipe the ocean floor with you."

SURFERS, BEWARE!

Shark computers take megabytes.

What did the sea captain say to the pop star?

"Please don't rock the boat."

And then there was the crooked merman who got arrested for starting a crime wave.

What is Corporal Octopus an expert in?

Hand to hand to hand to hand to hand to hand to hand to hand combat.

What military vehicle is found at the bottom of the ocean?

The fish tank.

Where does a clam go to lift weights?

Mussel Beach.

BOY: That building isn't a skyscraper. It's only a bait shack.

GIRL: But it has at least a hundred fish stories in it.

What do you get if you cross the ocean with a rabbit?

A wavy hare.

SEA OTTER: We need immediate assistance—we're starving.

SEAL: Relax. Kelp is on the way.

Why couldn't the little fish get a good job?

He dropped out of school before graduation.

—SHARK ATTACK—

What does a shark eat on its birthday?

Crab cakes.

What did the shark say to the bait?

"Hi, chum."

What does a shark do when it gets a sore throat?

It gargles with salt water.

MR. SHARK: I just came back from vacation.

MR. MARLIN: Where did you go?

MR. SHARK: Fin-land.

LOAN SHARK: Are you going to pay me in cash?

SHARKY: No. Here's a credit cod.

MR. SEA SPONGE RIDDLERS

Why did Mr. Sea Sponge go to the bank?
He wanted to float a loan.

What do you get if you cross a cabbage with Mr. Sea Sponge?
A vegetable that soaks its head.

How did Mr. Sea Sponge get past the crowd of tightly packed sardines?
He squeezed through.

Where does Mr. Sea Sponge buy his groceries?
At a fish market.

Why was Junior Sea Sponge's mom mad at him?
He came home from school soaking wet and dripped water on the floor.

TEACHER: Did you learn anything from my lecture today?
JUNIOR SEA SPONGE: No. You talked so fast, I couldn't absorb anything.

$E=mc^2$

Why did Mr. Sea Sponge go to Hollywood?

To visit his friend who is a starfish.

What does Mr. Sea Sponge use to call home?

A shell phone.

How does Mr. Sea Sponge cook a meal quickly?

He uses a microwave oven.

What did Mr. Sea Sponge say to his girlfriend?

"You're my main squeeze."

What does Mr. Sea Sponge do when he has a cold?

He takes in plenty of fluids.

Does Mr. Sea Sponge take a bus to work?

No. He goes by taxi crab.

How does Mr. Sea Sponge relax after a hard day?

He soaks in a hot tub.

What does Mr. Sea Sponge wear on his head?

A fishing derby.

Is Mr. Sea Sponge too chubby?

No. He just has a lot of water weight.

Does a flounder like sole food?

Do mermaids like to throw land parties?

What kind of fish can't keep a secret?

One that has a tattletail.

What kind of candy does the ocean eat?

Saltwater taffy.

Who makes the best seafood—fish or clams?

Fish can fry, but clams can bake.

What did King Neptune do in the stands at the baseball game?

He started a wave.

Who keeps King Neptune's castle clean?

The mermaids.

DAFFYNITIONS

Beach erosion: a case of bad tidings

Baiting the hook: a catchphrase

What kind of whales do you find off the coast of Scotland?

Kilt-er whales.

HA HA HA

Why do little fish like storms?

Because schools are closed during bad weather.

Why do fish make bad baseball pitchers?

Because they hate to be caught.

MERMAN: I visited a nightclub at the bottom of the ocean.

MERMAID: Was it a nice place?

MERMAN: No, it was a reel dive.

FISH #1: Why are you so dizzy?

FISH #2: Because I just took a tailspin.

Who is the dumbest whale in the ocean?

Moby-Dork.

What did the boy octopus say to the girl squid?

"Can I put my arms around you?"

Who guides a ship, is green, and has sharp teeth?

The navi-gator.

Where does a sardine go when it feels sick?

To the school nurse.

What did Mr. Fish wear to the office?

A bathing suit and tie.

MERMAID: Am I pretty or not?
MERMAN: Quit fishing for
a compliment.

WACKY BOOK REVIEWS

The Pearl—a gem of a sea tale

20,000 Leagues Under the Sea—
a book with a lot of depth

Moby-Dick—the sad tale
of a whaling ship

Mutiny on the Bounty—the revolting
story of an unhappy voyage

The Sea-Wolf—a biting sea story
that packs a punch

MR. BASS: I didn't see Mr. Tuna at work today.

MR. COD: He got canned yesterday.

Where does a fish farmer keep his tiny sea cow?

In a barn-acle.

MERMAN #1: Have you ever ridden on a dolphin by mistake?

MERMAN #2: No, but once I took a ride on porpoise.

MR. CRAB: What are your future plans?

MR. LOBSTER: To stay out of hot water if I can.

MINNOW: Why is the nurse shark visiting our school?

SARDINE: She's going to give us a herring test.

What did the bass yell to his friend at the intersection?

"Turn, pike!"

MARLIN: Why are you so grouchy? Is it something you ate?

SHARK: I'm not sure. I guess it could be the crab in me.

MINNOW: What is your favorite sport?
GUPPY: Bowl-ing.

ATTENTION!

Flying fish are found in high schools.
Smart fish know a lot about current events.

What's the easiest job in the ocean?

Being a lifeguard. Everyone there knows how to swim.

FISH #1: I'm riding the waves from England to France.
FISH #2: Oh, why don't you quit channel surfing.

DAFFYNITIONS

Sushi vendor: a sell-fish guy
Fishing show: reel-life TV

MAN: Hey! There's no bait on your line. What kind of fish do you expect to catch?
BOY: One that isn't hungry.

What do you get if you cross a fishing rod with Batman?

A reel superhero.

FISHERMAN: I caught this sea bass by accident.
CAPTAIN: For your information, it's just a fluke.

CHARTER BOAT CAPTAIN: Would you like to come fishing with us free of charge?
MAN: What's the catch?

SIGN ON A SHIPBUILDER'S FACTORY
Check out our sail items!

Knock-knock!
Who's there?
Eel.
Eel who?
Eel miss the boat if he doesn't hurry.

Show me a mate who swims through an oil spill . . . and I'll show you a sea-slick sailor!

MARTY: I went ice fishing.

ARTY: What did you catch?

MARTY: Frozen fish.

STARS OF
FISHING SHOWS

Rod N. Reel

Moe Torboat

Ivan Fishin

Annette S. Handy

MATT: I wrote a play about fishermen.

PAT: Can I be in the cast?

MATT: How are you when it comes to your lines?

PAT: Reel good.

Knock-knock!

Who's there?

I, Lloyd.

I, Lloyd who?

I Lloyd when I said I caught a big fish.

What did the little sea scallop say?

"I may be small, but I'm not a shrimp."

HA HA HA

2

PIRATE TREASURES

First Mate: Captain Morgan, I want my pay right now.

CAPTAIN MORGAN: Okay, but I'm short of cash. I'll have to give you a check, mate.

CAPTAIN MORGAN: Hey, matey! What's the name of that person floating in the ocean off the coast of Ireland?

FIRST MATE: Danny Buoy.

Why do basketball players make bad pirates?

They always jump ship.

Why did the pirate go to the eye doctor?

Arr, he kept seeing bleary treasure.

What did the pirate say to his beehives?

"Avast, bee hearties!"

Which nasty bug is a famous pirate?

Long John Silverfish.

What is a pirate's favorite fast food?

Pizzas of eight.

Who sails with Captain Niblet?

His buccaneers of corn.

How do pirates wash their clothes during a long voyage?

They sail with the Tide laundry soap.

How can you tell which treasure belongs to Super Pirate?

There'll be an *S* on his chest.

Which pirate got into trouble for not going to school?

Captain Hooky.

CAPTAIN: What do you see through that telescope?

FIRST MATE: A big ship with a lot of rabbits on deck.

CAPTAIN: It must be a hare-craft carrier.

DAFFYNITION

Walk the plank: a pirate's board game

Which tree is a famous buccaneer?

Barkbeard the Pirate.

What does Santa Pirate yell?

"Yo ho ho ho!"

What does a pirate say when he works in his garden?

"Yo hoe hoe hoe!"

What kind of strange noises did the pirate hear?

Ear-rings.

How did the pirate leader get a washboard stomach?

He did a lot of captain crunches.

Did you hear about the pirate captain who sailed his ship to the Arctic Ocean just so he could shiver his timbers?

Why did the lovesick pirate go to sea?

To search for his perfect mate.

Which pirate do fish fear the most?

Captain Hook.

Which sheep is a famous sea captain?

Sinbaa the Sailor.

What grades did the little pirate get on his report card?

Seven *C*'s.

3

COMPUTER CHUCKLES

What do you get if you cross a computer shopping service with cute lifeguards?

eBaywatch.

What sound does a computerized clock make?

Tech! Tech! Tech!

How do you send an electronic message to a beehive?

Use bee-mail.

ANN: I have a goose-feather computer.

DAN: What kind of computer is that?

ANN: One that makes it easy to *down*load stuff.

Where does a computer go
when it gets a virus?

To the .doc.

What did the computer
have for breakfast?

Spam and eggs.

What did the computer
whiz say to eBay?

"I don't need help, I'm just browsing."

Knock-knock!

Who's there?

Icon.

Icon who?

Icon hear you, so stop knocking.

What did the stressed-out computer say?

"I can't take disk anymore."

HA HA HA
HA HA HA HA HA
HA HA HA

ATTENTION!

Snobby computer users have their
own special cliques.

007: I know a spy who had an electronic device so tiny, he could hide it in his mustache.

008: What kind of device was it?

007: A liptop computer.

Where's the best place to find a donkey on the Internet?

Try eBray.

How do you catch a computer fish?

Use the Inter-net.

------- CHAT ROOMERS -------

Knock-knock!
Who's there?
M. T.
M. T. who?
M. T.-headed hackers.

Knock-knock!
Who's there?
I-M-A-B.
I-M-A-B who?
I-M-A-B keeper.
Buzz. Buzz.

Knock-knock!
Who's there?
C-N.
C-N who?
C-N is believing.

Knock-knock!
Who's there?
A-2-4-1.
A-2-4-1 who?
A-2-4-1 sale means big savings.

Knock-knock!
  Who's there?
N-E.
  N-E who?
N-E time S fine with me.

Knock-knock!
  Who's there?
U-R-N.
  U-R-N who?
U-R-N big trouble, dude!

Knock-knock!
  Who's there?
Co-M-E-D.
  Co-M-E-D who?
Co-M-E-D is funny stuff.

Knock-knock!
  Who's there?
R-U.
  R-U who?
R-U online?

Knock-knock!
  Who's there?
I-8-D.
  I-8-D who?
I-8-D whole cake.

Knock-knock!
  Who's there?
Z-S-4.
  Z-S-4 who?
Z-S-4 Zorro!

KNOCK-KNOCK!

Knock-knock!
  Who's there?
U-B.
  U-B who?
U-B good now.

What's the best way for a group of people to find something on the Internet?

Organize a search party.

How do you activate a chicken computer?

Cluck it on.

What did the computer masseuse send to her aching client?

An instant massage.

How do you buy a pet spider on the Internet?

Check out the web pages.

What is a computer's favorite type of music?

Disk-go.

What is a computer lover's wedding vow?

"I promise to love, honor, and eBay."

What do you get if you cross
a boxer with a computer whiz?
A guy who punches his
keyboard hard and fast.

What do you do if a computer
uses a bad word?
Wash out its speaker
with soap.

JILL: I'm tired of switching from site to site on
my computer.
BILL: Oh, you're surf-bored, huh?

What do you call a chicken who likes to
use a computer?
A technical fowl.

HA HA HA

ATTENTION!

Computerized robot dogs do not send flea-mail!

HA HA HA HA HA HA HA HA

Apple computer: the fruit of rapid growth in a high-tech industry

What does a hungry modem snack on?

Computer chips.

What does a hungry modem on a diet snack on?

Microchips.

IT'S A NUTTY WORLD

What did Oliver Twist say after he had lunch in Hawaii?

"Please, sir, I want Samoa."

What's green and sings?

Britney Asparagus Spears.

What did the bald customer say to the toupee maker when he called him on his cell phone?

"Can you hair me now?"

ALI: Aladdin was fortunate to find a magic lamp.
BABA: Yes—he has the luck of the I-wish folks.

Then there was the beaver that found a magic lamp and made tree wishes.

ALADDIN: What do you mean I have to pay airfare?
GENIE: Think of it as flying carpet tax.

Why did the jogger get a ticket?
  He ran a stop sign.

WHAT'S YOUR FAVORITE DAY?

15

"My burpday," said the soda pop.
  "Thirstday," said the camel.
"The Fork of July," said the spoon.
  "Stinksgiving," said the perfume.
"Valentime's Day," said the clock.
  "Earth Day," said the dirt farmer.
"New Ear's Day," said the cornstalk.
  "Presidentures' Day," said the dentist.

TRACY: My husband and I met while we were chasing a tornado.
STACY: Wow! Talk about a whirlwind romance.

AL: Do barbers read newspapers?
SAL: Yes but only the headlines.

How do you babysit a calendar?
Send it to a daycare center.

MAN: Why did you name your son Calculator?
FATHER: I wanted to be sure I could count on him in the future.

——— TIME TICKLERS ———

TED: My hound dog has fleas.
ED: Well, my watchdog has ticks.

JOE: What do you think of my new stopwatch?
MOE: Give me a second to think.

SIGN IN FRONT OF A WATCH-REPAIR SHOP
Around-the-Clock Repairs

Then there was the dumb boxer who punched the time clock and broke it.

CUSTOMER: Can I pick out any clock I want?
SALESMAN: Yes. Please, take your time.

My grandfather clock is so old, its time is running out.

ZACK: I think I should have bought that other watch instead of this one. I bet it keeps better time.
MACK: Oh, stop second-guessing yourself.

WHAT DID THE POLICEMEN SAY TO THE GANGSTER CLOCKS?

"Hands up!"

"Turn around slow and face me."

"I expect a confession any minute now."

"You got caught because you set off the alarm."

"No, I won't give you a second chance."

"If you know what's good for you, you'll tock fast."

"Now you'll wind up in jail."

"If you're lucky, you'll get time off for good behavior."

MAN: Do you have time for me today?
REPAIRMAN: No, sir. Your watch won't be fixed until tomorrow.

Show me an outdated skyscraper . . .
and I'll show you a building with lots of old stories.

JERRY: I'm going to be a famous stand-up comedian someday.
BARRY: Ha! Don't make me laugh.
LARRY: Yeah. Who are you trying to kid?

FIREMAN: The old glue factory just collapsed.
REPORTER: Is it a major disaster?
FIREMAN: No. But it's a very sticky situation.

LADY: What do you prescribe for my stuffy nose?
DOCTOR: Perfume.
LADY: What? Why perfume?
DOCTOR: It'll make you smell better.

—— SPEAK UP ——

MR. BATTERY: "I'll take charge!"
MR. LIGHT: "Say watt?"
MR. SCRAMBLED EGGS: "Beat it, dude!"
MR. CREDIT CARD: "Let's talk shop."

LOIS: I just saw Superman fly by.

JIMMY: Humph! Now there's a guy with no visible means of support.

NUTTY NOTICE

An archaeologist is a person who loves to live in the past.

What did one empty pyramid say to the other?

"I miss my mummy."

STRANGER: I'm looking for a town called Recovery.

FARMER: Turn left up yonder, and you'll be on the road to Recovery.

ZACK: What's wrong?

MACK: I just had a fender bender with a police car.

ZACK: Wow! Talk about a run-in with the law.

Ostrich: a chicken who spent years
in a bodybuilding program
Nutritionist: someone who knows
what's good for you
Buzz saw: a honey of a tool
Theory: a wise guy's hunch
Slowpoke: the punch of a tired boxer

SILLY SLOGAN

Cookbook publishers:
We'll show you some dish respect.

CHILD: Someone stole my snowman.
COP: This is a job for the cold-case investigators.

BOY: Do you always collect palm leaves?
GIRL: Yes, but I can take them or weave them.

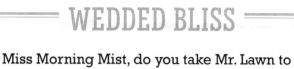

WEDDED BLISS

Miss Morning Mist, do you take Mr. Lawn to be your wedded husband?

I dew!

Who cleans up after the wedding ceremony?

The maid of honor.

Who married Mr. and Mrs. Broccoli?

The justice of the peas.

Mr. and Mrs. Bee went on a long honeymoon.

FATHER: My daughter, Melanie, cooks the dinner. My son, Matthew, pours the drinks. That's my son, Martin. He puts out the knives, forks, and plates.

GUEST: Oh, Martin is the setting son.

FATHER: Yes. He's my brightest child.

GIRL: Hooray! Hooray! Stir-fry those vegetables, Chef!

BOY: What was that?

GIRL: A wok-ing cheer.

HA HA HA

"Pass the bread," said the quarterback.

"Is this my plate?" said the umpire.

"Fork over the lettuce," said the robber.

"My glass is half full," said the optimist.

"My glass is half empty," said the pessimist.

"My steak is medium rare," said the psychic.

MIDDLE-EARTH
MIRTH

What vessel did the telephone pirates sail on?

The Fellowship of the Rings.

SARUMAN: Are you an expert at fixing doorbells?

SAURON: Yes, I'm the lord of the rings.

What do you get if you cross a rabbit with a small person from Middle-earth?

A hoppit.

Which rock-and-roll legend was in *The Lord of the Rings*?

Elvish Presley.

5

X-TREMELY FUNNY

What's the difference between the Easter Bunny and a great skateboard jump?

One's a big hare, and the other gets big air.

When does a witch ride on a motorcycle instead of a broom?

When she's competing in the Hex Games.

Show me a stunt rider who removes his wristwatch . . . and I'll show you an athlete whose timing is off.

What do you get if you cross a pop singer with a skater?

A rock-and-Rollerblader.

What do you call a pig on in-line wheels?

A skate pork.

Knock-knock!

Who's there?

Yemen.

Yemen who?

Yemen! That was a cool stunt, dude!

When are waves too small for surfing?

When they're microwaves.

What do you get when a Rollerblader doesn't shave?

A skatebeard.

When is the worst time to take a cross-country motorcycle trip?

During the fall season.

LADY: I rent a room in my house to a young man who roller-skates.

MAN: It sounds to me like you have a skateboarder.

MACK: Does Luke Skywalker use a lightsaber at the X Games?

ZACK: No, he uses a Rollerblade.

FRED: When did your pet dog learn how to skateboard?

ED: Right after the neighbor's cat learned how to roller-skate.

KEN: I met my new girlfriend at a skating park.

LEN: How did you two get together?

KEN: I saw her while I was riding my board and just fell for her.

BILL: What's the difference between a surfboard ride and a skateboard ride?

PHIL: Dude, fall off one, and you hear a big splash. Fall off the other, and you hear a big *crash*!

DAFFYNITION

Motocross: the wheel world

DON: My stunt bike is made out of wood instead of metal.

RON: What kind of bike is that?

DON: It's a tree-wheeler.

What did the clumsy skateboarder yell when he jumped in the air to perform a trick?

"Ollie-ooops!"

SPIKE: That motorcycle driver must be new to the sport.
MIKE: What makes you say that?
SPIKE: His bike has training wheels.

How do you get into a skate park for free?

Use a boarding pass.

How is Tony Hawk like an Olympic diver?

They both like to jump on a board.

Knock-knock!
Who's there?
Dairy.
Dairy who?
Dairy goes over the first jump.

6

ANIMAL ANTICS

Crow: Hey, raccoon! Why are you only eating the ears of corn at the bottom of the stalks?

RACCOON: I'm on a low-cob diet.

DON: Why isn't your watchdog at obedience school?

JOHN: I'm expecting unwelcome company, so he's taking a sic day.

What should you do if a goose has an accident?

Call in a parameduck.

JILL: Wow! How did you make your canary sing?

BILL: I gave it a piece of candy.

JILL: What kind of candy?

BILL: A special tweet mint.

Why was the bluebird mad?

He got a ticket for jaywalking.

Knock-knock!

Who's there?

Ewe.

Ewe who?

Now that's how a sheep yodels.

Who directs how and where rabbits drive their cars?

The hare traffic controller.

What does an alligator hear when he picks up the telephone?

The croco-dial tone.

CONNIE: How's the dog-grooming business?

DONNIE: It bites.

How does a veterinarian learn to cure ill cows?

He takes *moo*-sick lessons.

What does a New York Yankee zebra wear?

Pinstripes.

TIM: Want to hear a shocking story about a duck?

JIM: Sure.

TIM: Okay. Once upon a time there was a duck who had an electric bill.

What did the impatient racehorse say to the farmer?

"Quit trying to stall me."

POLICEMAN: You can't chew bubblegum in this neighborhood.

TEENAGER: Why not?

POLICEMAN: It's a no-popping zone.

What do you get if you cross an ATM with a dairy farm?

Lots of cash cows.

Greyhound trainer: a race-cur driver

Knock-knock!

Who's there?

Gillette.

Gillette who?

Gillette the dog out?

HA HA HA HA HA HA HA HA HA HA

MR. CROW: Bring me my new suit.

LITTLE CROW: What was that?

MRS. CROW: A clothes caw.

What's wooly, travels under the ocean, and goes *baa*?

An ewe boat.

Do rabbits lift weights?

No. They do hare-robics.

What do purple hens lay?

Eggplants.

Then there was the tough kangaroo who got a job as a nightclub bouncer.

ATTACK DOG TO TRAINER: I hate you. You make me sic.

ANN: I named my dog Magician.
JAN: Why? Does he do magic tricks?
ANN: Just watch. Magician, vanish!
JAN: Doggone!

NUTTY NOTICE

Invest in a pig farm and
put your fortune in good hams.

Which farm animal always cheats at hide-and-seek?

The Peking duck.

"I'm not interested in a gallop poll," said the horse.

"If you edit out my comments, I'll consider it a slop in the face," said the pig.

"I wish you wouldn't egg me on," said the hen.

"This is udder nonsense," said the cow.

What do you get if you cross a platter of fish with an egg-laying mammal?

A seafood platypus.

CRAZY QUESTION

Do business crows carry cawing cards?

Which tree supports animal rights?

The fake fir tree.

What do you get if you cross a turtle with a goose and the speed limit?

A slow-down zone.

Why did the lion king lose his golf match?

His opponent was Tiger Woods.

GHOSTLY GIGGLES

Why did the ghost haunt Albert Einstein for ten years?

It took that long to scare all the wits out of him.

GHOST: How did you like me in my last horror movie?
CRITIC: You were terrible! Horrible! Awful!
GHOST: Ah, it's nice to be appreciated.

How do computer ghosts contact each other?

Eeek-mail.

What is Little Dracula's favorite book?

The Bat in the Hat.

What's the main ingredient of spooky pizza?

Weird dough.

GHOSTWRITER: I penned a story about a vampire snowman.
GHOST: What's it called?
GHOSTWRITER: *Biting Cold*.

Why did the mad scientist name his monster Zero?

Because he was afraid of nothing.

What kind of weather do ghosts like?

Boo skies.

GHOST SAILOR: Is this haunted ship really manned by ghosts?
GHOST CAPTAIN: Yes. What did you expect, a skeleton crew?

What did the English ghost say after he accidentally scared King Richard?

"Frightfully sorry, sire."

HA HA HA
HA HA
HA HA
HA HA
HA HA

GHOSTWRITER NEWS

"My story is a haunting saga."

"RIP—Read It, Please."

"My doctor is mad about this book."

"You can really sink your teeth into the chapter about vampires."

"It has a killer cast of characters."

"I'm dying to write a sequel."

"My writing career was at a dead end until this book gave it new life."

"I hope it doesn't get buried in the bookstore."

WHAT DID THE CRITICS SAY?

"I'm afraid I don't like the burial plot."

"It has no shelf life at all."

"It has some grave editing problems."

"RIP—this book is so awful, it should be shredded and rest in pieces."

DAFFYNITION

Exorcism: the unspooken word

How do you build a haunted house?

Follow the boo-prints.

What did the sailor shout when
he spotted the ghost whale?

"Thar she boos."

What kind of ghosts live in magic lamps?

Boo genies.

Where does an unexpected guest ghost sleep?

On a fraidy-cot.

ATTENTION!

General Ghost tried to win the war by using scare tactics.

A ghost went to see a fortune-teller. "How are you?"
asked the ghost.

"I'm in good spirits today," replied the
fortune-teller.

What does a ghost use on his computer monitor?

A scream saver.

How do you spook a horse?

Show it a ghost.

What's soft and yellow and scary?

Winnie the Boo.

LADY: I saw a small ghost.
MAN: Was it a big shock?
LADY: No, but I was a little afraid.

WACKY WANT AD

Ghost actors needed—must be able
to perform before a live audience.

What do you get when a ghost vows not to speak?

Dead silence.

What fantasy creature is messy and scary?

The Slobgoblin.

Why are haunted houses always dark?

Ghosts scare the daylights out of them.

What does Jesse James's ghost wear on his head?

A cowbooey hat.

TIM: Are you really a ghost?

SPIRIT: I'm afraid so.

TIM: No, *I'm* the one who's afraid.

Knock-knock!

Who's there?

Cat's purr.

Cat's purr who?

Cat's purr the friendly ghost.

GHOST CAPTAIN: Are your men discouraged?

GHOST SERGEANT: No, sir! There's still some fright left in them.

What did the ghost sports fan sing on his way to South Bend, Indiana?

"Fright, Fright for Ol' Notre Dame."

ATTENTION!

Ghost soldiers don't crawl, they creep forward.

ATTENTION!

Before they can fly well, new vampires have to take batting practice.

The Wolfman likes to wear a houndstooth jacket.

Ghost fighter pilots fly phantom jets.

8

KNOCKING AROUND

Knock-knock!

KNOCK-KNOCK!

Who's there?

Brandy.

Brandy who?

Brandy-new gifts are my favorite.

Knock-knock!

Who's there?

Kobe.

Kobe who?

Kobe or not Kobe, that is the question.

Knock-knock!

Who's there?

Shaq.

Shaq who?

Shaq, rattle, and roll.

Knock-knock!
    Who's there?
Ewe.
    Ewe who?
Ewe go, girl!

Knock-knock!
    Who's there?
Oil.
    Oil who?
Oil have the blue plate special.

Knock-knock!
    Who's there?
Dish.
    Dish who?
Dish is the end of dish story.

Knock-knock!
    Who's there?
Wanda.
    Wanda who?
Wanda around, you'll find a place to camp.

Knock-knock!
    Who's there?
Soda.
    Soda who?
Soda Mets are finally in the World Series.

Knock-knock!
    Who's there?
Bean dear.
    Bean dear who?
Bean dear, done that.

HA HA HA HA HA HA HA HA

Knock-knock!
Who's there?
Milt Ed.
Milt Ed who?
Milt Ed cheese tastes good.

Knock-knock!
Who's there?
Yoda.
Yoda who?
Yoda one who makes my dream come true.

Knock-knock!
Who's there?
Egos.
Egos who?
Egos are big birds of prey.

Knock-knock!
Who's there?
Wits.
Wits who?
Wits the problem, won't your key work?

Knock-knock!
Who's there?
Heaven.
Heaven who?
Heaven you fixed this door yet?

Knock-knock!
Who's there?
Gwenyth.
Gwenyth who?
Gwenyth the train due to arrive?

HA HA HA

Knock-knock!

Who's there?

Hugh Carey.

Hugh Carey who?

Hugh Carey that suitcase, and I'll get this one.

Knock-knock!

Who's there?

Alma.

Alma who?

Alma money is tied up in municipal bonds.

Knock-knock!

Who's there?

Toupee.

Toupee who?

Toupee the admission price and the third gets in free.

Knock-knock!

Who's there?

Ooma.

Ooma who?

Ooma hand hurts from all this knocking.

HA HA HA HA HA HA HA HA

9

FUNNY BUSINESS

Mr. Green: My company produces live bait for fishermen all over the world.
MR. BROWN: What's it called?
MR. GREEN: Global worming.

Show me a group of people discussing insect hives . . . and I'll show you a bees' nest meeting.

Which secret agent works as a department-store Santa?

James Bond—Double Ho Ho Seven.

Which supercool spy cleans up after a snowstorm?

Austin Plowers.

Knock-knock!

Who's there?

Jewel.

Jewel who?

Jewel be sorry if you quit this job.

BUSINESSMAN: Let's form a committee to build a new dock.

BUSINESSWOMAN: Okay. I always wanted to be in a pier group.

WHY ARE YOU LATE?

"I got held up," said the banker.

"I was tied up," said the rope salesman.

"I was under the weather," said the meteorologist.

"I had car trouble," said the mechanic.

"I didn't get up on time," said the clock maker.

DAFFYNITION

Corral Enterprises: a company with a lot of stockholders

THE GAS HOUSE GANG

Phil Earup

Flip D. Hood

Anita Tuneup

Emanuel Transmission

MR. SMITH: What do you do for a living?

MR. JONES: I'm a salesman.

MR. SMITH: What does your wife do for a living?

MR. JONES: She's a saleswoman.

MR. SMITH: I guess that makes you two sellmates.

FOREMAN: Please remove all wristwatches before entering the factory.

NEW WORKER: Wow! I like this job. I just got here, and they're already telling me to take time off.

NUTTY NOTICE

People who sell flood insurance need
a dry sense of humor.

Then there was the chicken who got a job at a big hotel and worked as a desk cluck.

Then there was the CEO who loved surfing, so he took his board to the beach.

BOSS: If I put you in charge of the store, there's a lot to do. Can you handle it?
WORKER: Don't worry, I'll manage.

TINA: My money is in pork.
GINA: Hog farms?
TINA: No. Piggy banks.

Show me a man thinking about investing in real estate . . . and I'll show you a man with lots on his mind.

ZACK: I'm investing in a cattle ranch.
MACK: Now that's a bull market!

COMPANY PRESIDENT: It was a difficult decision to make. Thirty people applied for the job of vice president, and I could only pick one. I selected the best person for the job based on his outstanding qualifications. It's Mr. Jason Morgan. What do you say to that, Mr. Morgan?
MR. MORGAN: Yahoo! Thanks, Dad!

What do you get if you cross a guy who carries golf clubs with a seven-foot basketball star?

Caddy Shaq.

MAN #1: I work as a groundskeeper at a golf course.

MAN #2: Is it a difficult job?

MAN #1: It has its rough moments.

DAFFYNITIONS

Penny bank: a wee fund account

Crate manufacturers: case workers

WACKY WANT ADS

Hotel custodian needed—lots of rooms for improvement.

Person needed to fill salt-and-pepper shakers at restaurant—seasonal work.

Apprentice truck driver needed— before long, you'll be on the road to success.

HOME BUYER: I've looked at so many houses for sale, I'm starting to see double.
REALTOR: Nah! That's just a duplex.

What is the favorite game of sale items?
    Price tag.

CRAZY QUESTION
Do lumberjacks have to log on at work?

WORKER: What do you think of our new advertising campaign to sell jogging shoes?
CLIENT: I'm not sure. Run it by me again.

Knock-knock!
    Who's there?
Wade.
    Wade who?
Wade until tomorrow to ask for a raise.

HA HA
HA HA

SIGN ON THE SPORTS BANK
Our safe has a winning combination!

JOB HUNTERS

Become a hotel clerk—check us out.

Become a professional photographer—
picture yourself working for us!

Become a fitness instructor—this job is
guaranteed to work out.

Become a state lottery worker—this is the
chance you've been waiting for!

Mad doctor needed—teach an
anger management course.

BUSINESSMAN: Hooray! Hooray! Let's start
this meeting.

STOCKHOLDER #1: Who is that guy?

STOCKHOLDER #2: He's the cheerman of
the board.

NUTTY NOTICES

Invest intentionally, and you'll be glad you deed.

Invest in a trash compactor company—
buy junk bonds.

Invest in sugarcane—it's a sweet deal.

Invest in our road map company—we'll never
steer you wrong.

APPLICANT: What's it like to work here at the Ace Novelty Company?

PERSONNEL DIRECTOR: When it comes to making money, we don't joke around.

PETER: Do angels make good employees?

PAUL: Yes. They're miracle workers.

MAN: Where do you work?

WOMAN: At the wool sweater factory.

MAN: How is the union there?

WOMAN: It's a tightly knit group.

GET IT?

JOB DESCRIPTIONS

Babysitter—a person who changes frequently.

Gym teacher—a person who doesn't sweat it.

Mail carrier—a person who pushes the envelope.

LOONY LAWYERS

Mr. Will N. Testament

Mr. Hy Court

Ms. L. Sue Anybody

Mr. Manny Trials

Mr. Al Object

Knock-knock!

Who's there?

Reveal.

Reveal who?

Reveal we deserve a raise.

HA HA HA HA HA HA

WACKY WANT ADS

**People needed to clear snow—
take this job and shovel it.**

Snowplow drivers—make some cold cash.

10

THE MERRY MEDIA

What kind of television programs do yaks like?

Musk-see TV.

SAL: I'm watching an old tape of the Boston Marathon.
HAL: How can you enjoy viewing a rerun?

DIRECTOR: Doughnut Commercial.
BOX OF DOUGHNUTS: Take two!

HA HA HA

THE KOOKY TV CRITICS

"I question the value of TV quiz shows."

"There should be a law against violent police shows."

"Sci-fi shows just take up programming space."

"Reality shows are unreal."

FRIENDS OF THE METEOROLOGIST

Wayne E. Day

Cole Front

Sonny Mourning

Claire N. Coole

Tamara S. Better

SHOWTIME

The Pie Cooking Show—a slice-of-life program

The Ghost Cop Show—Law & Order S.V. Boo spinoff

Tornado TV—the real whirl

ACTOR: I'm the star of a new play called *Petty Theft*.

PRESS AGENT: Are you any good in it?

ACTOR: I steal every scene.

HOW DID YOU LIKE THAT NEW HOSPITAL SHOW?

"It made me sick."

"It needs an emergency rewrite."

"I don't have the heart to tell you."

"It was painful to watch."

"The leading man is such a bad actor, they should doc his pay."

"It's a bitter pill to swallow."

PRODUCER: How would you like to star in a television program about a commercial airline?

ACTOR: Oh, boy! A TV pilot at last.

ACTRESS: We named our new baby Channels.

REPORTER: Uh-oh! It sounds like the baby is crying.

ACTRESS: I guess it's time for me to change Channels.

NUTTY NOTICE

Atlas won an award for
Best Supporting Actor
for his role in *Mythology*.

ACTOR: I play a lumberjack in this movie.

REPORTER: What do you do in it?

ACTOR: I chop down trees.

REPORTER: When do you do that?

ACTOR: When the director yells, "Cut!"

What is the top TV quiz show in the Banana Republic?

Peel of Fortune.

DAFFYNITION

Mad TV: a place to channel your rage

Wacky game shows: loco broadcasting

JONI: I was hired to work on a soap opera.

TONI: Now's your chance to clean up your act.

AGENT: What type of act do you fellas do?

BOB: I sing.

ROB: I tell really dumb jokes and play stupid.

AGENT: Oh, you're a song-and-dunce team.

The Snake Show—E-Hiss-PN

The Farm Show—Hay-BC

The Ocean Show—Sea-BS

The Vegetable Show—Pea-BS

The Poultry Show—Hen-BC

FITNESS FUN

What did the tardy jogger say as he passed an old friend?

"I can't stop to talk, I'm running late today."

How do cattle stay in shape?

They exercise on a steer climber.

What did the angry baseball umpire shout to the bald coach?

"You're outta hair!"

What race did Seabiscuit win?

The Fishing Derby.

Which sports channel does a poultry farmer watch?

ESP-Hen.

Baseball star Swede Chariot went into the game to pinch-hit. The hurler for the other team was throwing knee-high fastballs. The hitter's coach yelled out this advice to his player: "Swing low, Swede Chariot!"

Where does a golf instructor work?

At a driving school.

Show me a businessman who produces blankets for football players who catch passes . . .
and I'll show you a guy who covers wide receivers.

Show me a hockey player with her skates on . . .
and I'll show you a slipshod athlete.

DAFFYNITIONS

Makeup artist: forgiving after an argument
Infield dirt: double playground
English wrestling champion: a lord of the ring
Decent golf player: a hole in two

What's the best way to ship a baseball hitter?
Put him in a batter's box and take him to the post office.

Show me a frog who plays basketball . . .
and I'll show you a player with a good jump shot.

HA HA HA

ED: Hey, Joe! What's foaming out of that soda bottle?
JOE: Relax! It's fizz, Ed.

MEL: Why are you so upset?
DELL: I want to run track, but when it comes to jumping the first hurdle, I'm afraid.
MEL: Relax, you'll get over it.

BOSS: Does Jack the custodian play on the company softball team?
COACH: Yes. He's our cleanup batter.

DAFFYNITION

Women's professional boxing:
beating men to the punch

WITCH: I put a hex on a golfer and he made a hole in one.

WIZARD: Is that par for the curse?

MAKING THE GRADE

Billy: I was a top student in bunk-bed school. How about you?

WILLIE: I was an undergraduate.

TILLIE: How did you learn to slow-cook a bunch of small fish?

MILLIE: I took a simmer-school class.

DAFFYNITION

The X-Files: the mystery of algebra

*Show me a geometry whiz ... and I'll show you a
student who thinks she knows all the angles.*

TEACHER: Today, we're going to watch a film
about exploring the ocean floor.
STUDENT: Oh, boy! A dive-in movie.

SILLY SLOGANS

Lumberjack school—if you come here,
try cutting class!

Ace Cooking School—our graduates
have to pass a taste test.

TEACHER: Do you like sewing class?

STUDENT: Yes. It's tailor-made for me.

SISTER: Did you do your addition homework on Thursday?

LITTLE BROTHER: No.

SISTER: Did you do your addition homework on Friday?

LITTLE BROTHER: No.

SISTER: Did you do your addition homework on Saturday?

LITTLE BROTHER: No. Why?

SISTER: Because Sum-day you'll be sorry.

SILLY SLOGAN

Lumberjack school tutor—if chopping homework has you stumped, ax for me.

BOY: My teacher doesn't know the difference between math and grammar.

MOM: What makes you think that?

BOY: She keeps talking about add-verbs.

7 + 6 = 13

TEACHER: Did you think band class would be all fun?

STUDENT: Yes. I only came here to play.

What do you get if you cross an art teacher with a math instructor?

A color-by-numbers project.

MAN #1: What's your line of work?

MAN #2: I'm a fence maker with a postgraduate degree.

BOY: How was my paper about the ocean? Was it good enough to get an *A*?

TEACHER: No, it was only *C*-worthy.

HEY, SUBSTITUTE TEACHER!

"Can you teach ancient history?"

"Sure. I have past experience."

"Can you teach gym class?"

"No sweat!"

"How are you at teaching geology?"

"Rock solid."

HA HA HA
HA HA HA
HA HA
HA HA

"Can you teach algebra?"

"No problem."

"Can you teach Spanish?"

"Just sí if I can."

"Can you teach English grammar?"

"Sure. It ain't hard."

13

COUNTRY SIDESPLITTERS

Show me a farmer with a bag of seeds in the middle of a city . . . and I'll show you a man with no place to grow.

POLITICIAN: How can we tell if farmers want to grow hay this summer?
ASSISTANT: Take a straw poll.

What rock-and-roll star plays guitar at the hive?
Johnny Bee Good.

What did one cool bee say to the other?
"Hi, pal! Give me a hive five."

Why did the farmer hire a schoolteacher?

He needed someone to grade his fruit.

FIREFLY: Ouch!

MOTH: What's wrong?

FIREFLY: Glowing pains.

FARMER: Son, tomorrow I want you to fertilize all the cornfields.

SON: Ah, Dad, that job stinks!

Knock-knock!

Who's there?

Gwen.

Gwen who?

Gwen do you milk the cows?

SILLY SLOGAN

Sheep farm—we believe in profit shearing.

NUTTY NOTICE

Young farmers are green recruits.

MAN #1: How did you get to the state fair?

MAN #2: I rode a hog.

MAN #1: You mean you rode a Harley-Davidson motorcycle?

MAN #2: No. I rode a hog. I'm a pig farmer.

Knock-knock!

　Who's there?

Garden.

　Garden who?

Garden sheep from wolves is dangerous.

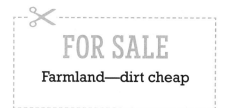

FOR SALE
Farmland—dirt cheap

Show me a shepherd who doesn't do a good job when the sun goes down . . . and I'll show you a man with a lot of sheepless nights.

SCIENTIST: We artificially produce this honey without the help of insects. How would you rate it?

FARMER: Bee-minus.

COUNTRY SINGER: My next song is called "How to Make Corn Grow Fast."

FARMER: That'll be music to our ears.

FARMER: How are we going to get all this hay in the loft before it rains?

FIELD HAND: Don't worry, we'll all pitch in.

FARMER: Are you here to paint bales of hay?

ARTIST: No, I'm here to draw straws.

What kind of car does a mad bull drive?

A snort utility vehicle.

Knock-knock!

Who's there?

I, Fred.

I, Fred who?

I Fred the chickens.

FARMER: I went to college to learn how to grow straw.

RANGER: Which college?

FARMER: Hay U.

Unclaimed baby sheep: no man's lamb

CITY FELLA: I thought farmers wake up early.

FARMER: Well, I always wake up before dawn.

CITY FELLA: Are you serious? It's noon and you just woke up.

FARMER: True, but Dawn is my wife, and she's still sleeping.

FARMER #1: That rooster always crows when he senses trouble.

FARMER #2: Maybe he's an alarm cluck.

SLIM: Did you hear about the two farmers on tractors who had a bad accident?

JIM: No. What happened?

SLIM: They plowed right into each other.

ATTENTION!

Invest in farm produce, and you can sit back
and watch your money grow.

What do you call a hen custodian?

A chicken super.

GRAPE GROWER: Did you hear the joke about the wine bottle?

FARMER: Yes. It was a real corker.

What's the dumbest fruit in the orchard?

The pear of idiots.

MAN: Phew! I spent the entire day picking small purple fruit.

FARMER: So?

MAN: Now I'm plum tuckered out.

HA HA HA HA HA HA HA HA HA

14

FEELIN' GOOD

Patient: What's the most important thing I need to know about my amnesia?
DOCTOR: Don't forget to pay my bill.

Knock-knock!
Who's there?
Destiny.
Destiny who?
Destiny that needs an operation, doc. The other knee is fine.

Aladdin became a doctor, and now, with the help of his magic lamp, he wishes people well!

NURSE: This patient is a kindergarten student with a slight temperature.

DOCTOR: Don't worry. It's just a low-grade fever.

PATIENT: I had to be out of my mind to come here.

PSYCHOLOGIST: Probably.

DOCTOR: I'd like to learn if you gained any pounds since you last visited me.

PATIENT: Okay. Where should I go?

DOCTOR: Back to the weighting room.

NUTTY NOTICE

Army doctors promote leg health, too!

DAFFYNITIONS

Pediatrician: a doctor who caters to a small group of people

Optometrist: a person you have to see

Pharmacist: a piller of the community

DOCTOR: Little girl, why are you sticking your tongue out at me? Are you sick?

LITTLE GIRL: No, I just don't like you.

What did the doctor tell the sick flower?

"Stay in your bed for at least a week."

DENTIST: Did you do well in medical school?

DERMATOLOGIST: No, I graduated by the skin of my teeth.

Why did the magician go to a chiropractor?

He had a trick knee.

DAFFYNITION

Doctor: someone who is sick of her job

HOSPITAL NURSE: What's wrong, captain? Are you feeling sick again?

CAPTAIN: No. I'm mad that they put me in a private room.

15

GIGGLERS' GRAB BAG

What kind of corn do they grow in Texas?

Texas Range-Ears.

What do they say at the dinner table in New Hampshire?

"New Hampshire tastes better than old ham."

Which colleges do smart plants attend?

Ivy League schools.

ATTENTION, SOLDIERS!

"Fall in," said Major Swimming Pool.

"Hop to it," said Captain Kangaroo.

"Present arms," said Sergeant Biceps.

"Eyes right," said Lieutenant Optometrist.

"Fall out," said Colonel Balding.

"At ease," said General Comfort.

FOR SALE

Tunneling equipment—
far below cost.

Which silly state is best known for long baseball hits?

Oklahomer.

Which fish plays soccer?

The goal fish.

Show me a grumpy meteorologist who dates a grouchy weather girl . . . and I'll show you a stormy relationship.

Knock-knock!

Who's there?

Rio.

Rio who?

Rio funny, wise guy. You know it's me.

KNOCK-KNOCK!

IT'S A BEAUTIFUL WORLD

"I have no ill feelings," said the doctor.

"It's a grate day," said the cheese grinder.

"I could jump for joy," said the basketball player.

"Everything is in perfect harmony," said the leader of the chorus.

WIFE: Did you remember to bring home a bag of ice?

HUSBAND: No, dear. It slipped my mind.

RABBI: What is that heavenly smell?

MINISTER: It's scent from above.

HA HA HA HA HA HA HA HA

BOOK AUTHORS

How to Collect Overdue Bills by Cindy Money

The Story of Archery by Beau N. Harrow

The Jogger's Handbook by Ron A. Round

How to Tell Dumb Jokes by Stu Pitt

SILLY SONG

"As Long as You Take My Temperature"
by Justin Fever

What did the river say to the ocean when the salmon arrived?

"I can't talk now. My mouth is full of fish."

Which royal bird was a merry old soul?

Old King Crow.

CAL: I'm on a jump rope diet.

HAL: What kind of diet is that?

CAL: One that makes it easy to skip eating between-meal snacks.

SCIENTIST: I failed nine times at making a perfect cat robot, but this time I know my little robot will be a success.

REPORTER: What do you call this robot?

SCIENTIST: Kit-ten.

BYE-BYE

"I'll catch you later," said the bounty hunter.

"I'm outta hair," said the bald guy.